AWESOME HEROES

by Rosie Peet

DK | Penguin Random House

Senior Editor Tori Kosara
Editor Rosie Peet
Senior Designer Anna Formanek
Designer James McKeag
US Proofreader Kayla Dugger
Pre-production Producer Marc Staples
Producer Louise Daly
Managing Editor Paula Regan
Managing Art Editor Jo Connor
Publisher Julie Ferris
Art Director Lisa Lanzarini
Publishing Director Simon Beecroft

First American Edition, 2019
Published in the United States by DK Publishing
345 Hudson Street, New York, New York 10014

Contents

Meet the heroes

Six heroes live in a city called Apocalypseburg. They are Emmet, Lucy, Batman, Benny, Unikitty, and Metalbeard.

Batman

Emmet

Lucy

4

The city used to be a fun place to live. Now, it is in ruins.

Metalbeard

Benny

Unikitty

Under attack

Aliens destroy the city again and again. They stomp through the streets. They knock over buildings. They even eat bricks! The city is a mess.

Lucy

Lucy is a brave hero. She wants to stop the aliens. When the aliens destroy something, she helps build it again. Lucy thinks that she always needs to be tough.

Lucy is not afraid of the aliens.

How to be tough

Lucy has created rules about how to survive in Apocalypseburg.

DO
1. Wear dark colors
2. Look tough
3. Drink black coffee

DO NOT

1. Sing cheesy pop songs
2. Be too cheerful
3. Try to make friends with the aliens

Emmet

Emmet is Lucy's best friend. He is always cheerful, even when everyone else is gloomy. Not even the aliens can make him sad! He always knows how to cheer Lucy up.

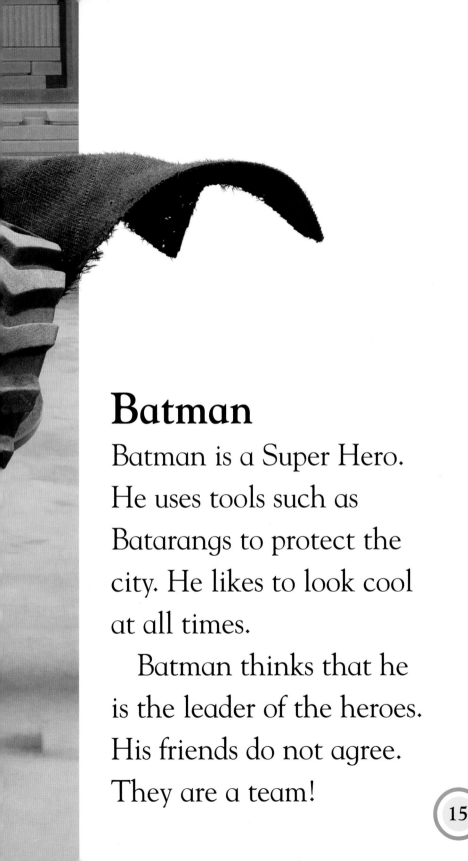

Batman

Batman is a Super Hero.
He uses tools such as
Batarangs to protect the
city. He likes to look cool
at all times.

Batman thinks that he
is the leader of the heroes.
His friends do not agree.
They are a team!

Unikitty

Unikitty loves happy things. It is hard to be happy when aliens attack! Sometimes, Unikitty gets really angry. When she does, she turns into fierce Ultrakatty. Aliens, watch out!

Unikitty

Ultrakatty

Benny

Benny is an astronaut. He is great at building, just like his friends. His favorite things to build are spaceships. He gets very excited whenever anyone talks about spaceships!

Benny uses ball-shaped weapons to defend the city.

Metalbeard

Metalbeard is a fearless pirate. His body is made out of pieces of ships. His legs are made of swords and a telescope. He is ready to stop the aliens!

Rex

Rex is a space pilot. He is super cool and he knows it! He explores the universe in his spaceship. It is called the *Rexcelsior*. A team of dinosaurs called raptors helps him on his ship.

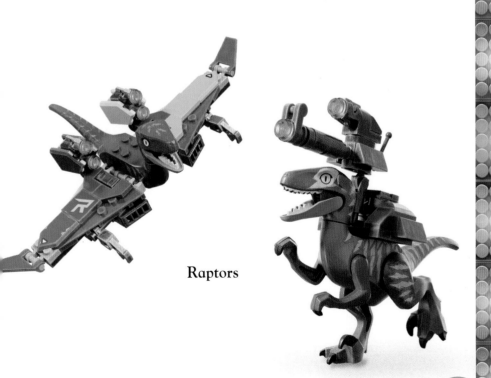

Raptors

On the road

Every hero needs a cool way to get around the city. Here are some of their awesome vehicles.

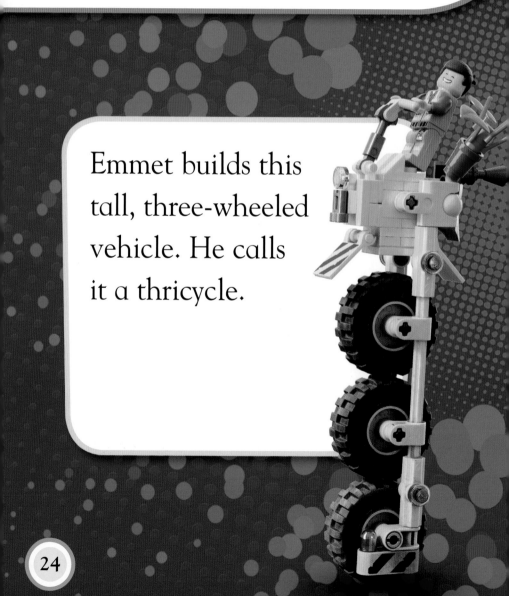

Emmet builds this tall, three-wheeled vehicle. He calls it a thricycle.

Emmet and Lucy build this getaway car to escape from aliens.

Clever Metalbeard can turn his body into a bike. He just adds wheels!

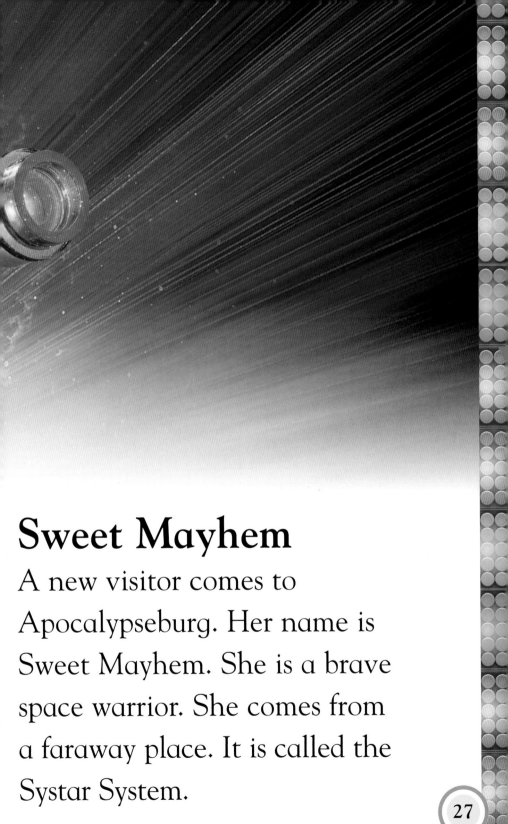

Sweet Mayhem

A new visitor comes to
Apocalypseburg. Her name is
Sweet Mayhem. She is a brave
space warrior. She comes from
a faraway place. It is called the
Systar System.

The *Formidaball*

Sweet Mayhem has a spaceship called the *Formidaball*. It is shaped like a ball.

Door

Cannon

Missiles

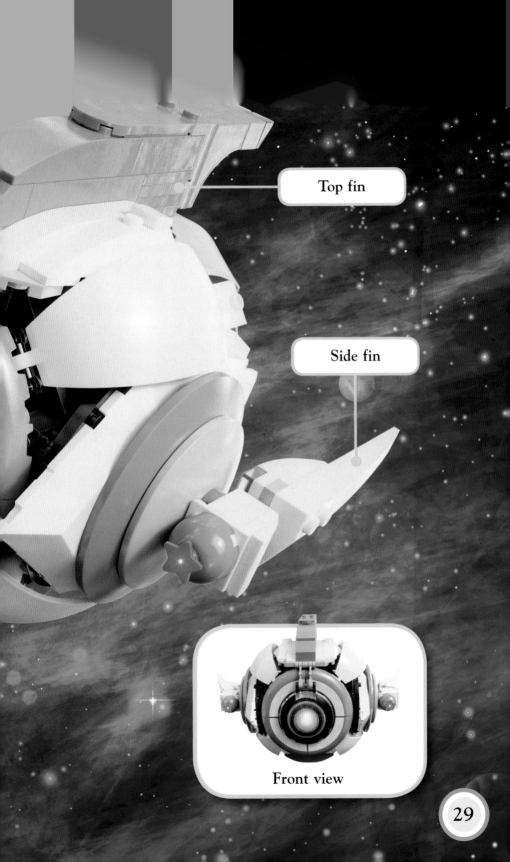

Top fin

Side fin

Front view

Blast off!

Sweet Mayhem wants to take Lucy, Batman, Unikitty, Benny, and Metalbeard to the Systar System.

She takes them into the *Formidaball.* They blast off into space. Benny is excited to be inside a spaceship!

Royal welcome

The friends have arrived in the Systar System. It is the home of Queen Watevra Wa'Nabi.

The Queen can transform into whatever she wants to be! The heroes think this is very cool.

Ice Cream Cone

Ice Cream Cone is the Queen's
butler. He helps the Queen with her
plans. Ice Cream Cone always keeps
a cool head, no matter what.

The Queen and Ice Cream Cone

Spa time

The Queen sends the heroes to a special spa. They need to be cleaned up!

The spa is awesome. Everything is clean and sparkly. Happy pop music plays loudly. Unikitty loves it here!

Plantimals

Emmet and Rex also come to
the Systar System. They look for
Emmet's friends.

They meet some Plantimals.
These creatures look cute, but they
are very dangerous!

Dangerous beasts

Emmet thinks the Plantimals are cute. He tries to pet one of them. It becomes angry! Rex gets caught in a Plantimal's long vines.

Rex and Emmet run away to find Emmet's friends.

New friends

Emmet is happy. He has found his friends! The heroes cannot wait to explore the Systar System together. They want to find out more about the creatures who live here. Maybe they can all be friends.

Quiz

1. Where does Lucy live?

2. Which hero thinks he is the leader?

3. Who does Unikitty turn into when she is really angry?

4. What are Benny's favorite things to build?

5. What is Metalbeard's body made of?

6. Where does Sweet Mayhem come from?

7. What is the name of Sweet Mayhem's spaceship?

8. Who is the Queen's butler?

9. Who loves the spa?

10. Which cute-looking animals are really dangerous?

Answers on page 47.

Glossary

astronaut
A person who explores space.

defend
Protect something from attack.

destroy
Ruin or break something.

telescope
A tool you look through to see
things that are far away.

transform
Change into something else.

vehicle
Something you can use to travel,
such as a car or a bike.

Index

Answers to the quiz on pages 44 and 45:

1. Apocalypsburg 2. Batman 3. Ultrakatty 4. Spaceships 5. Pieces of ships 6. The Systar System 7. The *Formidaball* 8. Ice Cream Cone 9. Unikitty 10. Plantimals

A LEVEL FOR EVERY READER

This book is a part of an exciting four-level reading series to support children in developing the habit of reading widely for both pleasure and information. Each book is designed to develop a child's reading skills, fluency, grammar awareness, and comprehension in order to build confidence and enjoyment when reading.

Ready for a Level 2 (Beginning to Read) book
A child should:

- be able to recognize a bank of common words quickly and be able to blend sounds together to make some words.

- be familiar with using beginner letter sounds and context clues to figure out unfamiliar words.

- sometimes correct his/her reading if it doesn't look right or make sense.

- be aware of the need for a slight pause at commas and a longer one at periods.

A valuable and shared reading experience

For many children, reading requires much effort, but adult participation can make reading both fun and easier. Here are a few tips on how to use this book with a young reader:

Check out the contents together:

- read about the book on the back cover and talk about the contents page to help heighten interest and expectation.
- discuss new or difficult words.
- chat about labels, annotations, and pictures.

Support the reader:

- give the book to the young reader to turn the pages.
- where necessary, encourage longer words to be broken into syllables, sound out each one, and then flow the syllables together; ask him/her to reread the sentence to check the meaning.
- encourage the reader to vary her/his voice as she/he reads; demonstrate how to do this if helpful.

Talk at the end of each book, or after every few pages:

- ask questions about the text and the meaning of the words used—this helps develop comprehension skills.
- read the quiz at the end of the book and encourage the reader to answer the questions, if necessary, by turning back to the relevant pages to find the answers.